Strange Plants

Monica Halpern

Contents

Plants Are Important

Did you know that you couldn't live without plants? Plants provide much of the **oxygen** that people and other animals breathe. Plants provide much of the food they eat, too.

Plants are living things that can do some amazing things. Most plants make their own food. They grow everywhere. They keep on growing until they die.

Plants come in all sizes and shapes. Some have colorful flowers. Others have no flowers at all. Some are so tiny that you need a **microscope** to see them. Others are taller than giraffes.

◀ These plants grow in a tropical rain forest.

Plants come in lots of colors, shapes and sizes because they live in many different places. They live in wet swamps and dry deserts. They live on cold mountaintops and in lush river valleys. They have **adapted**, or changed, so that they can **survive** in the places in which they live.

Unlike animals and people, plants can't move around. Most are rooted in one place. But they still need to **protect** themselves from their enemies. They also have to find a way to get water and **minerals**, or food.

Many plants have developed interesting ways to find food and to protect themselves from their enemies. Some produce **poisons** to keep animals from eating them. Others have sharp thorns that scratch animals that get too close. Still others catch and eat animals!

Let's take a look at some of these amazing plants.

Lavender and lichens ▶
grow in a mountain range
in Mongolia.

Did You Know?

Scientists have discovered more than 350,000 species, or kinds, of plants.

◀ This tall, spiky cactus grows in dry desert areas.

These giant ▶ lilies grow in a forest.

Meat-Eating Plants

Of the hundreds of thousands of different kinds of plants in our world, only about 400 eat meat. Most of these plants grow in wet places like swamps, marshes or bogs. The soil in these places is poor. It doesn't have enough minerals to keep plants healthy. So these meat-eating plants have adapted over time. They get the minerals they need by eating animals.

Meat-eating plants are too small to eat large animals. Most of them eat insects. But a few eat mice, frogs and even small birds.

All meat-eating plants do some things in the same ways. They offer a special treat, or **bait**, to attract animals. They catch the animals in some kind of trap. Then they **dissolve** the animals into a kind of soup. Finally, they **digest** the soup.

The butterwort plant ▶ feeds on insects.

The cobra lily is a meat-eating plant that lives in swamps.

7

Venus Flytraps

One of the best known meat-eating plants is the Venus flytrap. It offers its victims a sweet treat. A sugary liquid covers its leaves.

Insects smell the sweet liquid. They crawl onto the leaves. They expect a delicious meal. Instead, tiny hairs on the leaves know the insect is there. These hairs act as **triggers**. SNAP! The leaves snap shut. The closed leaves form a cage. The insect can't escape.

The sides of the trap start to press together. Within 30 minutes, the insect is squashed and killed. Then the trap fills with liquid. Over a week or two, most of the insect's body dissolves into a kind of soup. The plant eats its meal. The leaves then open again. They are ready for the next meal to arrive.

Did You Know?

Of all the strange plants, the Venus flytrap is the most popular. People like to have them as houseplants.

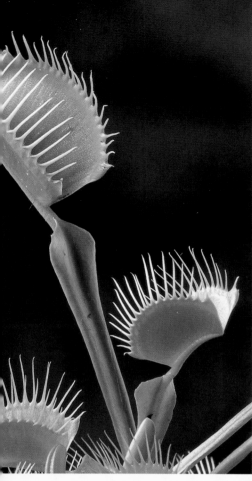

▲ The open leaves of a Venus flytrap attract insects.

▲ When a fly lands, it triggers the leaves to trap shut.

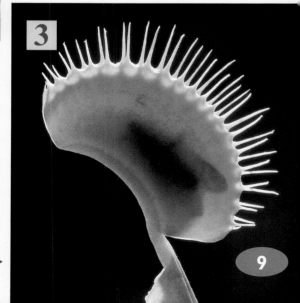

The fly is trapped inside. ▶

Bladderworts

The tiniest of the meat-eaters is the bladderwort. It may be small, but it can still catch tiny insects. It does this by sucking them up!

Most bladderworts live in or around water. They float in lakes and ponds. Some bladderworts even live in puddles.

The bladderwort's leaves have what look like tiny bubbles on them. These are the bladders. They catch and digest the victims. Some bladders are so small you need a microscope to see them.

Each bladder has a trapdoor. There are tiny hairs near the trapdoor. If an insect touches some of the hairs, the trapdoor suddenly opens. WOOSH! The victim is sucked into the bladder. The trapdoor snaps shut. The animal is trapped. This happens faster than the eye can see.

The bladderwort plant ▶
floats in water.

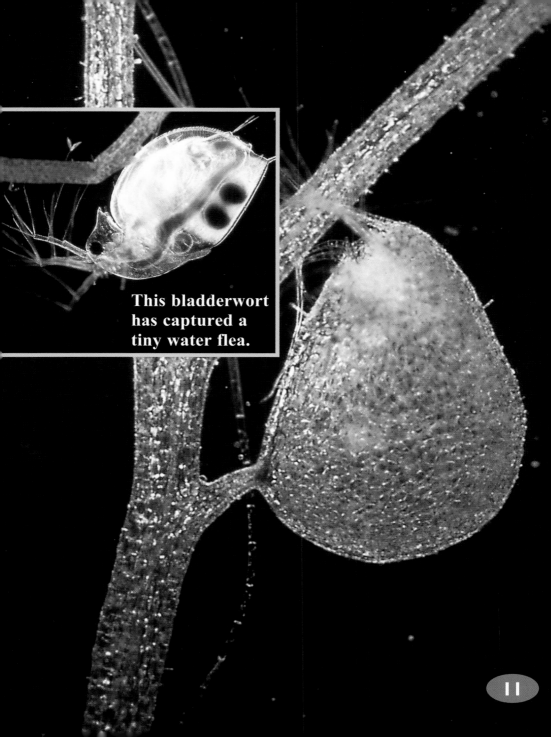

This bladderwort has captured a tiny water flea.

Pitcher Plants

Unlike bladderworts, pitcher plants have no moving parts. They drown their victims. Some pitcher plants are tiny and catch only small insects. But in some parts of the world, pitcher plants are large enough to catch mice, lizards, frogs or even birds.

The pitcher plant's leaves are shaped like a **pitcher**. Many are brightly colored, with bright red streaks along the top. The leaves have a sugary liquid along their edges.

An insect flies by. It sees the colorful plant and smells something sweet. It lands and tries to suck up the liquid. But the sides of the leaves are steep and slippery. The insect slips and slides down them. At the bottom of the pitcher is a liquid that the plant makes. The insect falls into the liquid and drowns.

The plant digests the soft parts of the insect. Only its **skeleton** is left. Sometimes a pile of skeletons collects at the bottom of the pitcher plant.

◀A spider crawls along the top of a pitcher plant. Soon it will slide down inside and drown.

Sundew Plants

Sundew plants trap insects on their sticky leaves. The leaves are covered in fine hairs. Each hair has a drop of sticky liquid at its red tip. The drops gleam in the sunlight like morning dew. That's where the name of this plant comes from.

When an insect lands on a leaf, it sticks to a hair or two. It struggles to free itself, touching more sticky hairs. The nearby hairs bend over the insect and hold it down.

Once an insect is caught, the plant produces a juice. It pours this juice over the insect. The juice turns the insect into a soup. The plant eats the soup.

Sundew plants never pour their juices onto anything but food. If a piece of sand lands on a leaf, the plant will not produce any juice.

The hairs of a sundew ▶ plant bend over to trap an insect.

Did You Know?

The sundew plant is used as flypaper in some parts of the world.

14

Poisonous Plants

Unlike meat-eating plants, poisonous plants can hurt or even kill people. These plants make poisons to stop their enemies from eating them. Anything that eats these plants will become sick and may die. That includes you!

Most poisonous plants taste **bitter**. It's one way to keep animals from eating them. Like you, most animals don't like bitter foods.

Some poisonous plants use chemicals to keep their enemies away. These plants sting any animal that brushes by them. If you brush against some of these plants, you may get a painful **rash**. Other poisonous plants will actually prick you with their poison. They work like a doctor's needle.

Did You Know?

Hundreds of years ago in Italy, murderers gave their victims gloves dusted with a poison made from the monkshood plant. The poison entered the victim's body through cuts or scratches on their fingers.

The monkshood plant ▶ is one of the most dangerous poisonous plants. Tiny amounts of its poison can kill.

▲ The henbane plant is a smelly, poisonous plant found in Great Britain.

Poison Ivy

"Leaves in three, let them be." Remember this saying. It's a reminder to stay away from poisonous plants like poison ivy. These three-leaf plants grow as climbing vines or low plants. They often grow along the side of roads or next to forest paths.

When you're out on a hike, look out for these shiny, pointed leaves. They contain a sticky oil. If you brush against them, the oil **oozes** out onto your skin. You might feel the sting first. Or, a few hours later, your skin might start to itch. Ugly, red blisters will appear. The rash can last for weeks. Don't scratch! You'll only spread the rash.

You can get a rash from poison ivy even if you never touch the plant. People can get it by touching dogs or other animals that have brushed against these plants. Its oil can even be spread by garden tools, picnic things, or anything that has touched the plants.

Watch out when you see a plant with three leaves like this. Poison ivy can make you break out in an itchy rash.

Stinging Nettles

Other poisonous plants have weaker chemicals, but a stronger sting. Their poisons don't just ooze out. These plants put their poisons right into the skin of any creature that comes near.

The stinging nettle stings any animal that touches it. The leaves of the stinging nettle are covered with millions of tiny, hollow spikes. The spikes are filled with **acid**. The tips of the spikes are like glass. They break off when they are touched. What is left of the spike is very sharp.

If you happen to brush by a stinging nettle, its spikes will cut your skin. Acid will flow into the cut. Then you'll get a hot, painful rash. Usually the rash will go away after an hour or two. But some people suffer for a day or more.

The sharp spikes on a stinging nettle are filled with acid.

Did You Know?

The stinging nettle is sometimes grown on farms. The plant produces a strong fibre that is used to make a type of cloth.

Amazing Plants

Plants really are amazing. The plants you have been reading about have developed special ways to survive. They have found ways to protect themselves from their enemies and to find food.

Scientists are still discovering new facts about plants. They know that some plants can help fight disease in people. These plants are used to make medicines. So far, scientists have studied only a tiny number of all flowering plants. We can only guess what amazing facts about plants they will find next.

Foxglove is used to make ▶ a drug to treat people with heart conditions.

Glossary

acid   a substance that can burn your skin

adapt   to change to fit new conditions

bait   something used to attract another animal

bitter   an unpleasant taste

digest   to break down food into a form the body can use

dissolve   to mix with a liquid

microscope a tool used to look at very small objects

mineral   an element needed by plants and animals

ooze   to leak out slowly

oxygen   a gas that animals need to survive

pitcher   a large jug

poison   a substance that can make you ill

protect   to keep safe

rash   an irritation of the skin

skeleton   the bones of an animal

survive   to keep living

trigger   something that causes something else to happen

Index